Every
Mother
Can Keep
Her Cool

Every
Mother
Can Keep
Her Cool

Julie Barnhill

Revell

a division of Baker Publishing Group
Grand Rapids, Michigan

© 2008 by Julie Barnhill

Published by Revell
a division of Baker Publishing Group
P.O. Box 6287, Grand Rapids, MI 49516-6287
www.revellbooks.com

Printed in the United States of America

ISBN 978-0-8007-1908-1

Published in association with the literary agencies of Alive Communications,
Inc., 7680 Goddard Street, Suite 200, Colorado Springs, Colorado 80920, and
Fedd & Company, Inc., 9759 Concord Pass, Brentwood, Tennessee 37027.

As women, we hold within our grasp
the power to change the world.

One family at a time.

One mother heart at a time.

We **don't** have to run for political office.

We **don't** have to write books.

We **don't** have to tell a hundred thousand
people the details of our journey.

No,

we can make all the difference

simply

by telling the truth of our life.

To ourselves first . . . then to **one another**.

Do you find yourself feeling

hot under
the collar,

irascible,

huffy,

sore,

in**cen**sed,

aggravated,

indignant,

chafed,

exasperated,

furious,

ed,

piqued,

riled,

maddened .

and dealing with anger?

Just between you and me—

each word of experience, prayer, insight, gentle warning, and real-life proof of lasting change mentioned within these pages was first tested and lived out (for better or worse) in my own family relationships as a mom.

You are not alone. Thousands upon thousands of women have shared with me personally via conversation, email, phone calls, or handwritten letters that, yes, even tough mothers struggle with matters of anger, feeling blue and depressed, fleeting humor reserves, and stress.

The truth is, it isn't so much about getting everything right. Who among us reading these pages could honestly claim to have done that as a mother anyway? The important thing is acknowledging specific matters in our life as a mom for which we desperately need and desire change. And I can't think of anyone more willing and able to step up and do just that than me. So relax and stay awhile as we take a closer look at anger and discover inspirational and practical tools to deal with it.

By telling your story, there will be times you are the lifeline for another mother.

You will be the saving grace for her children.

And you will be the reason that mother is able to believe she truly isn't alone.

Years ago, in fits of uncontrolled anger, I acted out and spoke harshly and irresponsibly to my two oldest children (now ages twenty and eighteen). And I thought even worse things than I said.

I had no idea my children could and would provoke in me such visceral anger. *My children* being the operative term because I had always known other people's kids drove me crazy. It's one of the main reasons—well, it was *the* reason—I never spent much time babysitting as a teenager or college student.

But I was the adult now.

The adult mom of two very wanted children.

Yet over time, increasing emotions of tension and irritation gave way and raging, boiling, uncontrollable anger spewed verbally from my mouth and was also vented physically against my kids.

I was a mess and despised the mother I had become. So I did what I always used to do those many years ago; I jumped in my car and went to the nearest bookstore in the hope of finding the book to solve all my problems. I even approached a store manager and asked, "Where is your section for moms who really, really, really wish they had never had children?"

"There is none," he responded.

"There should be," I grumbled back.

And it seemed, no matter how many stores I visited (remember, this was in the prehistoric ages before amazon.com or google.com), I never could find what I kept referring to as a "real" book regarding anger, motherhood, and children.

Oh, there were lots of texts telling me what anger was and even more telling me I shouldn't be feeling and expressing it as uncontrollably as I did. Lots of scholarly type stuff but nada from a living, breathing, female author expressing what I so desperately needed to hear: "I was out of control in my anger and found a way to change." Instead, I read words and first-person experiences that came across a bit more like this: "I was once so mad at my child that I could just spit!"

Uh, that wasn't helpful in the least.

So it was then—way back in the early nineties—I determined that if I should ever make my way out of that volcanic place of mothering, I would write and speak of the things no one wants to say—let alone admit—for public consumption.

These pages are written in the hope that you will read and discover, perhaps for the very first time, that someone else has been exactly where you are right now—or where you fear you may be going if something doesn't change.

My confessions are made so you might know there is hope for change—long-lasting, redemptive change. Anger doesn't have to have the final word in your heart or in your home.

And here's even more profound truth: no matter what you've said, what you've done, or what you've thought, none of it is beyond the power of God to forgive, restore, and redeem.

Not one part of it.

So stop right here at this place in the book and think of your own list of confessions regarding anger and your life as a mom. Don't be afraid to face those memories, words, thoughts, and actions. They are what they are, and ignoring them isn't going to change the past or help you respond differently in the future.

Now, concerning each memory, speak this truth (out loud if at all possible):

It's what I said or did or thought.
It's not who I am.

And you know what? It's true!

Your angry words, actions, or thoughts do not have to define you as a mother. You do not have to live beneath the condemning weight of an angry moment or angry past. And do you know why? Because the truth of who you are as a mother supersedes it all.

Truth #1: You love your children
and know right from wrong.

I've spoken with tens of thousands of mothers over the past ten years, and I've never, ever come across a mother who didn't recognize and acknowledge that what she was doing in her anger was wrong. I've never had to cajole said mothers or convince them of their guilt. No, each one of these mothers who shared their story knew—just as I knew years ago—when they had gone too far.

Neither have I met a mother who confessed, "I don't love my child." However, and this is so important for you to read and digest, I have met and held mothers who whispered in agony, "How can I love my children and be such an angry mother?"

I asked myself this question and wrote it in my journal more than seventeen years ago. Hours before, I had angrily thrown my just-under-two-year-old daughter onto her bed, and her tiny body hit the bedroom wall.

I wanted to vomit.

I wanted to run away as far as possible to protect my daughter from . . . *shudder* . . . her mother. From me!

I cried uncontrollably (the crinkled journal pages testify to my shame and regret even now) and dared to write the following:

"Is it possible I don't love my child?"

If you have been there, my sweet friend, or fear that you will be as you struggle with increasing levels of frustration, anxiety, anger, and yes, even rage, I ask you to hold this book even tighter and repeat the following:

I am not alone.

Please know that the author of this book has been in the parental muck when it comes to getting mad (and acting irrationally). I know what it's like, and the entire purpose of writing this book is to assure you that there is another mom who has known exactly what you're dealing with and struggling against.

You are not alone.

Take hope in this and repeat these truths again:

I love my children.

It's what I've done. It's not who I am.

And add the following:

I will no longer continue to live this way.

Truth #2: You have created "ruts of behavior" when it comes to anger, and it's going to require concerted effort on your part to change.

Make no mistake, it can and will happen if (*if!*) you'll submit yourself to change and begin implementing self-control and self-restraint in all things pertaining to your buildup of anger. And I really believe it's important for you to realize that God has to play a big part in this if change is going to happen. Without apology, I believe that apart from God supernaturally changing our hearts as mothers—apart from Him getting into our business and uprooting and highlighting internal matters—we cannot experience lasting change.

I've stated this truth before in previous writings and believe it's worth repeating yet again.

When my heart changes, my thoughts change.
When my thoughts change, my words change.
When my words change, my actions will always follow.
And it is then and only then
that I find lasting change as a mother.

There.

I said it. And it feels good having done so.

You may agree or disagree, but I'm convinced that you can buy this book or a hundred others like it, and if your heart does not change by the sheer power and ability of God, nothing concerning your behavior will change for the duration.

I believe this, for I've seen it happen in my own life as well as in the lives of thousands of mothers. It's not "Julie Power," or "The Power of the Positive Thinking Mother." It is the power of a gracious and kind God who delights in bringing life and joy and laughter back into hearts and homes. And by such grace and power working in and through you, change will come.

Truth #3: You're not about to give up
or give in.

Whew! Keep hanging on, mothers! Don't give in and
don't let up in your dogged pursuit of a more peaceful parenthood. You can find lasting change. You can
enjoy (there's a concept!) your children and smile as
you consider what lies ahead.

You cannot tell from appearances how things will go.

Sometimes imagination makes things out far worse than they are. . . . This is the lesson:

Never give in.
Never give in.
Never, never, never, never—in
nothing, great or small,
large or petty—never give in,
except to convictions of honour
and good sense.

Never yield to force;

never yield to the apparently over-whelming might of the enemy.

Sir Winston Churchill

A strong emotion;
a feeling that is orientated
toward some real or
supposed grievance.

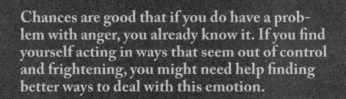

Chances are good that if you do have a problem with anger, you already know it. If you find
yourself acting in ways that seem out of control
and frightening, you might need help finding
better ways to deal with this emotion.

from *Controlling Anger—Before It Controls You*
The American Psychological Association*

*Accessed online at http://panicdisorder.about.com/cs/shanger/a/
angerhelp.htm, December 2007.

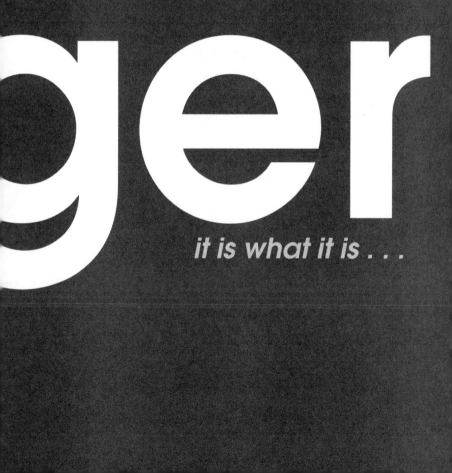

We boil at
different
degrees.

Ralph Waldo Emerson

ger

it is what it is . . .

Know How She Blows

Everyone has a style of erupting when it comes to anger, and the sooner you identify yours the better. Now, bear in mind, it is entirely possible to have more than one style. In fact I'd go so far as to say most of us erupt differently at different times . . .

Depending on the hormone levels coursing through our bodies.

Depending on varying outside circumstances factoring into our day.

Depending on which child stepped on our last frayed nerve!

All these contribute to the anger buildup. And it's important to recognize these contributing factors, as well as know how you finally blow it. The best visual I've ever come up with likens our outbursts of anger to that of a volcanic eruption. Think of yourself as Mount Momma and consider your style of blowing it:

Hawaiian: The molten rock of this volcanic eruption will often seethe away in the center of its crater, doing little damage, until sooner or later the fiery lava boils up in the crater and flows over the sides. Usually the lava flows slowly—giving people ample time to get out of its way.

Hawaiian Mother Eruption: Despite her rather innocuous appearance, a mother erupting in the Hawaiian style specializes in chronic, simmering anger. You may look calm and relatively cool on the outside— and to the gaze of others—but you know your insides are often twisted up into knots or you struggle, perhaps, with an overall down or negative view of life.

Fallout from Hawaiian Eruptions

caustic criticism
negative assessments
unfavorable comparisons
guilt trips
poor follow-through
pessimistic tendencies

Strombolian: When this volcano blows it on the tiny island of Stromboli, Italy, it sounds a lot like a powerful jet engine at close range. Volcanic materials are spit out with the force of the eruption: cinders and thick and pasty lava bombs. The eruptions are relatively short and sweet and, oh, so predictable. So much so, in fact, that they're often considered one of the least threatening of volcanic eruptions. But Mount Mommas everywhere know better.

Strombolian Mother Eruption: I was a Strombolian mom in those early years. My eruptions were predictable and short-lived, and I liked to think the residual damage was minimal. But I was wrong.

Fallout from Strombolian Eruptions

verbal cinders of sarcasm
regret
loss of respect for self for demonstrating
such lack of self-control
nearly nonexistent laughter and joy in the home

Vulcanian: This ain't your momma's Hawaiian-style eruption! Pent-up molten rock churns beneath the surface until blobs of viscous (read: thick and pasty) magma are expelled in a big, gassy explosion. Nice, huh? This one is loud and ugly, girls. Clouds of ash-laden gas, steam, and solid volcanic rock are ejected from the mountaintop. And that gas! Whew, that gas will literally kill you as it sucks the oxygen clean away from your lungs. Clearly, you don't want to be around a Vulcanian eruption if you can help it.

Vulcanian Mother Eruption: A Vulcanian explosion produces shrapnel—verbal, physical, and emotional—that can shred the spirits of a woman's children and the safety of her home. Objects may be thrown along with poisonous words—including insults and accusations—and actions such as slaps and shakes. Such wrath is often unpredictable and may repeatedly be aimed at a particular child. The Vulcanian eruption finds a mother engaged in willful and increasingly harder-to-stop behavior. Reasonable, self-checking thoughts are increasingly harder to hear and act on.*

Fallout of Vulcanian Eruptions

verbal shrapnel
physical shrapnel
emotional shrapnel
poisonous words
increasingly difficult to control (or desire to stop)

Plinian: Think Mount Saint Helens, circa 1980. The Plinian is the most violent of volcanic eruptions. The sheer volume of material ejected by the eruption sets it apart, and its violent explosive power can literally change vast physical and geographical landscapes. The explosion of 1980 and its subsequent fallout cost 57 people their lives. Over a 22,000-square-mile area, an estimated 1.4 billion cubic yards of ash fell.

---

*See Julie Barnhill, *She's Gonna Blow! Real Help for Moms Dealing with Anger* (Eugene, OR: Harvest House, 2001), 40.

Plinian Mother Eruption: Erupting like this as a mother is extreme, explosive, and, yes, can even be life-threatening. You know if it's happened; and if it has, you're all too familiar with the consequences. Let me speak directly regarding this reality: if you find yourself fighting (and losing) the battle against such dangerous emotions and actions, seek professional help and counsel immediately. Such volatile behavior puts your family in danger physically and mentally. (You'll find some resources listed on page 68.) Do not allow shame and fear to stop you. Some mothers have expressed to me worries of what will occur if they tell someone. I've responded each and every time the same, "What will happen if you do not?"

Fallout of Plinian Eruptions

really losing it—screaming until you're hoarse, possibly cursing
rampaging through your house
perhaps even physically beating a child
saying the kind of things that kill a child's spirit
feeling emotionally and physically spent afterward

Whew.

You've just read some pretty heavy material and may be tempted to close the book at this point. It can be overwhelming, seeing the reality of your anger build-up described on paper with no disclaimers or excuses.

But I beg you not to turn away or avoid the reality of anger's grip on your mothering life.

Instead, choose to face truth. Choose to acknowledge and take ownership of your explosive emotions. And choose to take whatever steps are needed to find lasting change and healing for you and your family.

It all starts with taking note of what it is that tends to set you off.

That Really Hacks Me Off!

Our children bring us incredible joy, yet there are times they bring out incredible anger in us. And it's not just our kids—there are any number of situations, circumstances, events, and adult interactions that raise our hackles. It is helpful to identify the experiences that provoke and trigger your anger so you can make positive changes in your household. Here are some examples cited by real mothers just like you and me.

Toddlers

They can be, oh, so adorable most (or at least some!) of the time, but our toddlers also have a way of making us just a little crazy some days. Consider the following:

Leaking sippy cups

Toilets and nonflushable items

Naptime battle of wills

Hypersensitivity to the toe seams in their socks

Crayons, markers, and Sharpies on the walls

A possessive streak that makes playing with other toddlers so much fun

Messy fascination with mud puddles in the church parking lot

That "Me do it! Me do it!" mantra that's only cute for the first two seconds

Need I say more?

This too shall pass . . .

Favorite blankies,
Temper tantrums,
Potty training,
Chutes and Ladders,
Big-boy underwear,
7:00 pm bedtime,
Toddlerhood.

Childish Behavior

Okay, I know you're not supposed to act the way I do as a mother—especially when it comes to handling a three-year-old, but sometimes I get so angry at the mess this child makes again and again. Technically I know this is just part of her being a child but when I look at the toys and the stuff everywhere . . . well, I definitely find myself getting irritated and snappy.

Alicia

Oh my, have I ever been there! I remember a time during a February snowstorm in 1996 when my middle son, Ricky Neal, decided to go running through our darkened (the electricity had been knocked out) house. I told him not to do it. I told him to stop. I told him if he got hurt, I wasn't going to feel sorry for him. He got hurt (it involved a small gash on his eyebrow and ridiculous amounts of blood). I got angry and yelled, and it wasn't until his father was driving him to the nearest ER (thirty minutes away) that my ramped up irritation (bordering on anger) began to subside.

Kids will be kids, they say. And we know it's true. But when we're in the thick of childish realities, it still manages to get under our skin sometimes, doesn't it?

Teasing and Goading and 'Tude . . . Oh My!

My son is on this teasing kick. He takes great pleasure in getting me riled up. This may or may not be a preteen thing. I try not to get upset. He pulled it this morning real bad. I work a twelve-hour shift, and he got me so worked up, I didn't know how I would be able to concentrate on work.

Carol*

I have a four-year-old and two-year-old twins . . . do I really need to say anything more?

Janice

My daughter is sixteen and no one does attitude like this child! Every morning my husband and I look at each other and wonder if Ms. Jekyll or Ms. Hyde will come stomping down the stairway. But here's the thing: she "does" attitude without saying

---

*Barnhill, *She's Gonna Blow!* 28.

a word . . . it's just there, in her gaze, in her stance, and she can take me from peaceful to hacked-off in 0.6 seconds.

Laura

Ah, yes, a child's arsenal of nonverbal attitude is loaded with such weapons as The Gaze (not to be confused with The Eye Roll) and The Stance, and fortified with volleying verbal refrains against sibling and mother alike. It's amazing (pathetically so at times) how quickly we allow such demonstrations to hack us off or set us off altogether. This is the time to hunker down and keep your emotions and responses cool and collected. After all, you are the adult.

Whacked-out Schedules

Our overly busy schedules tend to hinder our efforts to remain calm and collected. I pulled the plug on schedule overload sometime around my youngest child's seventh birthday. I had realized that if I didn't do something different—drastically different—I and/or my husband would be running three children to various activities and locations four out of five nights a week. Ugh. Neither one of us wanted that, so we made a new family rule: each child had to choose one extracurricular activity.

Kristen dropped basketball; Ricky chose not to participate in junior league football, and Patrick joined one traveling basketball team rather than the two available for sign-up. As a result, the Barnhill family was less spent financially and physically, and their mother found it easier to relax, enjoy, and cheer at the activities she did attend.

This too shall pass . . .

Parent-chaperoned field trips,
Piano practice,
Dance recitals,
Multiplication tests,
Goodnight kisses,
Childhood.

Hormones (Ours and Theirs!)

Oh, what a number hormones can play on our propensity to lose our temper! Shifting moods, headaches, cramping, bloating, and just not feeling our best can contribute to our blowing it. One of the best things you can do for you and your child is to teach him or her to respect this very real and very female reality. Don't worry; it won't require your spilling the beans on everything.

Just start simple and keep it succinct.

Pick up one of those fun magnetic mood indicators and stick it to your refrigerator door. Highlight the facial expression that best summarizes how you feel around breakfast and tell the children they've been forewarned if it's a "Don't Mess with this One Tough Mother" day—or month!

"Momma's bloated, back off!"

I spoke those exact words to my boys as they were growing up, and that pretty much said what needed to be said. Believe it or not, they really did back off and often attempted to tone down what I perceived at the time as extremely annoying behavior. I never mentioned ovaries or menstrual cramps nor did I use my bloating as a crutch. I simply wanted the boys (and their sister) to respect the fact that I was indeed female—as hard as it was for them to comprehend.

Our female hormones make possible our greatest gifts—for only we can bring forth life. But hormonal lack or imbalance can also be our most consistent enemy, causing the all-too-common miseries that can accompany PMS and menopause.

Scientists don't know exactly why women get PMS or why some women experience it more severely than others, but they believe that it stems from a combination of hormonal changes, genetics, nutrition, and psychological factors. Some of the most common psychological and physical symptoms include:

Mood changes (crying for no reason, depression, anxiety, anger, sadness, or irritability)

Changes in mental functioning (inability to concentrate or remember)

Changes in sex drive (increased or decreased libido)

Upset stomach, diarrhea, or constipation

Fatigue

Difficulty sleeping

Headache

Fluid retention and bloating

Acne

Breast tenderness

Joint or muscle pain

Cramping

Food cravings (especially for carbohydrates, chocolate, and other sweets)

Weight gain

The good news is, there are things we can do to alleviate PMS symptoms.

Diet

Take care of your body by adjusting your diet.

Do consume:

Calcium supplement with vitamin D

Complex carbs

Daily multivitamins

Don't consume:

Alcohol

Caffeine

Nicotine

Simple carbs

Exercise

During a workout, levels of chemicals called beta-endorphins rise. These chemicals impact mood and behavior positively. Experts say that exercising at least three times a week can reduce anger and depression and fight stress during PMS.

Stress Reduction

Although stress doesn't cause PMS, it can worsen its symptoms. Implement relaxation techniques that can help you calm down and relax. Consider picking up a copy of *Every Mother Can Let Go of Stress* and apply some of the suggested "soul-utions" for stressed-out moms.

Medications

When diet, exercise, and stress reduction aren't enough to alleviate symptoms, medications may be needed. Over-the-counter medicines, such as those containing acetaminophen (Tylenol) and ibuprofen (Motrin), can relieve cramping and other minor aches and pains. Some medications are marketed specifically to women experiencing PMS symptoms. These medications, which include Midol and Pamprin, typically include a combination of aspirin or acetaminophen for pain, plus diuretics. Diuretics prevent water retention to relieve bloating.

It's Not Just Us—They Have Them Too!

Don't forget about your children's hormones—hormones do contribute to instability of mood, particularly around the ages of ten, eleven, and twelve. After that, things seem to settle down hormonally around age thirteen. Hormones can account for some mood instability around those ages, but after that other factors take over—such as the sheer significance of their physical development. Remember these important factors and re-familiarize yourself with some common emotional development touchstones when handling your preteens.

Often preteens feel awkward and insecure because of the physical changes they are undergoing. Take a minute and think back to your middle school years. *Shivers!* Keep those memories in mind when you're facing a pugnacious twelve-year-old who seems inordinately preoccupied with his looks. Because he is!

Most preteens rely on their friends for their needs and feel drawn to belonging to a group. It isn't uncommon for parents to feel as if their child's friends have usurped the family's central place in her life. It happens in the majority of families but isn't necessarily easy to accept. (Been there, done that three times.) Just remember how up and down these friendships can be at this age—thick as thieves one day, sworn enemies the next. Hang in there and just be the mom. They need you now more than ever before as they move through the turbulent waters of peer acceptance and rejection.

Preteens test limits and challenge rules—especially your rules. All of a sudden, your thirteen-year-old has an opinion about everything and he doesn't hesitate to spew it. Hold him to the standard of respectful parent-child communication (if you haven't taught this to your child yet, now is an excellent time to do so) and learn from one of my biggest mistakes—don't make every moment a "teaching" moment. Often fewer words are best.

Preteens can act a lot like toddlers. Enough said—almost. It's really important to remember this reality. Even though your daughter may wear the same size shoe as you, her ability to reason and act responsibly, well, not so much. You may find your twelve-year-old son surpassing you in height (both my boys had by this age), but height doesn't equal mature thinking processes. Our preteens crave and often demand independence yet expect us to take care of them:

"Why didn't you wake me up in time for breakfast?"
"Can I have some money to buy you a gift?" Sound
familiar?

Preteens want to be left alone—but in a heartbeat
can plop themselves down next to you on the couch
and cozy up like a toddler. *Sigh*. I love it when that
happens.

The planning and organizational skills of preteens
are not well developed (here, take a look at my son
Patrick's room if you don't believe me) and they are
masters of making excuses for what didn't get done.
Oh, and they're not so good with time either. Always
quantify what they mean when they answer, "Later."
That could be in two minutes or two months.

This too shall pass . . .

Braces,
Curfews,
Raging hormones,
Sleepovers,
Empty fuel tanks,
Voracious appetites,
Friendship drama,
Tuxedo fittings,
Proms and homecoming,
Teenhood.

And Finally . . . the Real World

Financial worries. Work responsibilities. Fears.
Addictions. Depression.

Too much to do and too little time.

Migraines, muscle aches, and sheer exhaustion.

Life's not always a cakewalk, and there are days
when the balancing act stretches us past our limit. The
house is a mess, the kids are acting out, and there's no
relief in sight. It's no wonder we're a little on edge.

So how do we keep from falling off that edge?

So don't lose a minute in building on what you've
    been given,
complementing your basic faith with good
    character,
spiritual understanding,
alert discipline,
passionate patience,
reverent wonder,
warm friendliness,
and generous love,
each dimension fitting into and developing the
    others.
With these qualities active and growing in your
    lives,
no grass will grow under your feet,
no day will pass without its reward as you mature
    in your experience of our Master Jesus.
Without these qualities you can't see what's right
    before you,
oblivious that your old sinful life has been wiped
    off the books.

2 Peter 1:5–8

Reading the Signs

There are warning signs and signals for nearly everything that can possibly harm you: tornado sirens, food packaging labels, train whistles, tsunami alerts. So too there are signs that your mounting frustration is ready to morph into flat-out anger. Numerous physical warnings can help you discern what's really going on in time to quell anger's buildup:

Tense muscles

Holding your breath or shallow breathing

Feeling as though your body temperature is rising (it probably is!)

Increasing feelings of frustration, disappointment, fear, or panic

Flushed face and a burst of energy caused by a rush of adrenaline

When you find yourself experiencing even one of these warning signs, stop immediately and ease your emotions by trying some of these healthy and non-crazy-mom suggestions:

Concentrate on your physical reactions.

Remind yourself to breathe! It's common to hold your breath as anger builds. Inhale deeply—slowly concentrating on the flow of air. Exhale fully and completely.

Relax your facial muscles—pay attention to those furrowed eyebrows and pinched lips. Work your jaw and even place your hands to your face and massage the tension building along your forehead and jawline.

Make a point of also paying attention to emotions other than anger. Often one or more of the following feelings are precursors to possible build-up of more volatile expressions of anger:

Impatience
Discontent
Irritability
Depression
Disappointment

When you feel one of these emotions taking over, stop and acknowledge it verbally: "Okay, I can tell irritability is really starting to crank up, so I need to be very careful not to allow it to build or feed an angry outburst or thought." Then *choose* to stop it from feeding an issue of anger. Seems dorky? Well, perhaps it is, but I'm telling you, if you truly want to change your angry responses, it's one of the simplest and most effective ways to get there. Never underestimate the power of self-control.

Post this at all the intersections, dear friends:

> Lead with your ears,
> follow up with your tongue,
> and let anger straggle along in the rear.
> God's righteousness doesn't grow from human
> anger.

James 1:19–20

It's never too late to tell your children you're sorry.

There's nothing more powerful than a mother asking forgive-

ness for her angry outbursts.

As long as you're breathing—there's time.

Things to Do instead of Yelling

Put your hands over your mouth (in other words, keep
your mouth shut).

Do not speak or move toward your child until you have
cooled down and are in control of your words and
actions.

Stop in your tracks. *Drop* your tense shoulders and con-
sciously release tensed muscles. *Breathe* deeply.

Count to 10 or 20 or as long as it takes you to simmer down.
Learn how to do this in Spanish—preferably, learning with your children—and concentrate on each syllable and inflection. Choose to take your anger out on *uno, dos, tres,* rather than on your child.

uno ("OO-no," just like the game)

dos (like a "dose" of medicine)

tres (the *r* is pronounced with a flip of the tongue tip against the roof of the mouth. I can't do this and I'm part Spanish!)

cuatro ("KWAH-tro")

cinco ("SINK-oh")

seis ("SAYSS," rhymes with "trace")

siete (roughly "SYET-tay" with the first syllable rhyming with the Russian "nyet")

ocho ("OH-cho," rhymes with "coach-oh")

nueve (roughly "NWEHV-ay," with the first syllable rhyming with "Bev")

diez ("dyess," rhymes with "tress")

Phone a friend. There is one small caveat, however. Unfortunately, few of us have corded phones any longer. Most of us are talking on our cell or cordless home phone, and this means we can stomp around and even follow after the child who is pushing all our buttons! This isn't such a good thing to do, especially in the midst of our attempting to dispel our frustration with a friend. If you choose to reach out and touch someone, commit your feet to a stationary position and let your friend talk you down from there.

Take a hot bath, splash cold water on your face, or simply utter a guttural, "Aurggggg!" Trust me, this feels great and it helps you expel otherwise pent-up negative energy. It is what it is, so give yourself permission to get your angries out creatively and safely.

Pick up a pencil (now, now, don't throw it!) and write down your thoughts. Here's another peek at my journal from years gone by:

> AURGGGG! I am SO ANGRY right now I just want to SCREAM! I'd probably rip the roof off the house and send every toddler in this neighborhood running to their calm mommies. AURGGG!
>
> I don't understand eight-year-old boys at all. Why does my son insist on climbing trees that are thirty feet tall? Why does my son do everything full-throttle? Has the boy never considered taking things easy? Maybe thinking a step or two ahead? If I don't have a heart attack before his ninth birthday, it will be a miracle.
>
> I just want to quit. Q. U. I. T.

My dear brothers, take note of this:
Everyone should be quick to listen,
slow to speak and slow to become angry,
for man's anger does not bring about the
righteous life that God desires.

James 1:19–20 NIV

Four Questions Every Mother Needs to Ask

1. Am I expecting too much for my child's age?

Sometimes I wonder if we spend more time trying to figure out our newest iPhone than we do studying our children and learning what makes them tick. Two of the best things you can ever do as a mom are:

- identify the individual temperaments of your child and yourself
- know the characteristics of the developmental stages of children (birth through eighteen years)

Two excellent resources are: *Personality Plus for Parents: Understanding What Makes Your Child Tick** by Florence Littauer, and an excellent online summary of developmental stages written by Elaine Gibson at http://www.elainegibson.net/parenting/develop ment.html. (Hundreds of mothers have contacted me

---

* Florence Littauer, *Personality Plus for Parents: Understanding What Makes Your Child Tick* (Grand Rapids: Revell, 2000).

and thanked me for including both these resources in my first book, *She's Gonna Blow! Real Help for Moms Dealing with Anger*.)

2. Do I always say no?

Okay, I wrote an entire chapter about this in *One Tough Mother*,** and I'm not about to step back from my conviction that mothers must be able to say no without apology or guilt. I don't want you to lose any healthy confidence when it comes to being the boss. But I also believe it's always wise to look at what we're doing and to evaluate the strengths or weaknesses of our actions.

To that end let us consider how easy it is to get into a rut of not listening and simply blurting out no in response to any request. Needless to say, doing so over and over and over again can contribute to a messy cycle of frustration on your child's part—and not unmerited frustration either.

** See Julie Barnhill, *One Tough Mother: It's Time to Step Up and Be the Mom* (Grand Rapids: Revell, 2007), 79–97.

So, think about how often you say no. Are you consistent with the important ones? Do you perhaps need to listen a bit longer to what your teenager is asking? And what tone and inflection does your voice carry when you say no? All of these questions are worth your time and consideration. Tweak what needs to be tweaked and if it's not broke, well, leave it alone.

3. Am I a thermometer or a thermostat?

Years ago author and speaker Donna Otto challenged me and about three thousand other mothers to be a thermostat as a mother; to "set the temperature" of our home rather than simply "registering the tone and temperature," as a thermometer would do.

Her words have shaped my mothering for nearly twenty years now. The imagery was just what I needed as a twenty-something mother. I was convinced and convicted that I would no longer hold my family hostage to my feelings, but rather would set a tone of peaceful calm for all of us.

Granted, I've blown my top a few times over the years, but time and time again I have come back to this truth. So, Mom, what are you doing in your home—simply registering the emotional and relational chaos or confidently setting a tone for all to follow?

4. Have there been major changes in our home or lives?

Does it ever amaze you how clueless you can be about your own life sometimes? I'm going to let you in on a little secret. It wasn't until I was writing a particular chapter in a book of mine (um, I'm talking ten-plus years after the fact) that the lights went on and I realized how stress-filled my first few years of marriage and family were. In that aha! moment I literally laughed out loud, shook my head in doofus amazement, and said to myself, "Well, no wonder you were such a mess, Julie."

How about you? Take a few minutes and look back on the past days, weeks, months, and years. Have any of the following occurred?

Death of a spouse

Divorce

Marital separation

Detention in jail or other institution

Death of a family member or close friend

Marriage (and/or remarriage)

Losing a job/being fired

Pregnancy

Miscarriage

Gaining a new family member (adoption, foster care, older adult moving in, and so on)

Major change in financial situation (a lot worse or better off than formerly)

Major change in arguments with spouse (often dealing
    with children)

Taking on a mortgage or foreclosure of a home loan

Outstanding personal achievement

Child leaving home

Change in residence

Any one or an accumulation of above circumstances could be contributing to your struggle with
anger. Don't read any further until you have taken the
time to weigh such matters and perhaps have your
own aha! discovery.

LORD,

How I wish things could just settle down for a while.

It seems as though each day, week, and month all but guarantees a change that my children and I have to adjust to.

You know, sometimes I just wish things could remain the same as they are right here, right now.

Everything isn't perfect—not by a long shot.

But at least I know what to expect today.

Tomorrow seems to bring only promises of more change.

Sometimes it's hard to pray. I know with my head that I am to trust You—"only trust" You, as an old hymn used to go.

But trust lives far from me more days than not.

So I will choose—willfully choose to do it anyway!

I will trust You.

I will continue to come to You with all my stuff.

I choose You.

Changing One Day at a Time

As I'm writing these last few pages, my two sons (ages eighteen and thirteen) are actually sitting in the living room playing a video game together. Thus far there's been no verbal sparring or bruise-inducing punches to one or the other's arm or thigh. (Mothers of boys will understand this completely.) Our entire home is relatively anger free and that, my friend, is no small miracle.

Over the past fifteen years, I have implemented skills and techniques to get the upper hand with the often volatile emotion of anger. See, most of the time in those early years, my anger built up over a period of days and centered on miniscule happenings. I had to reroute my thinking out of the rut it was in and change long-seeded behavior.

Incremental change after incremental change over the course of days, months, and yes, even years, allowed me to get ahead of both small everyday frustrations and more deeply entrenched individual problems. Sticking with it helped to prevent big ugly blowups until one day—literally one day out of the unexpected blue—I realized I no longer reacted emotionally, verbally, and physically, as I once had.

I was a changed mother and I felt great. This is my desire for you as well, that you may come to a place of unshakable contentment and relational security as the great mother of your children. Please know that it will take time. Anything worthy of time and value always does. So don't grow disheartened. As you identify your "Mount Momma" type and take a closer look at what is setting you off, you're going to see change—hear change—and feel change in the core of who you are as a mom. As you persevere (never give in, remember?!) and choose not to give in to discouragement you'll find consistent change—day to day and year after year.

Remember that feeling angry isn't "wrong." Expressing your anger in excessive, inappropriate, unproductive, and hurtful ways is.

Change your demands into desires. Accept—really accept—the fact that you're going to have to give. You can't have everything your way. So often this needed change goes against every preconceived notion we have of being a perfect mother. But guess what? There is no such person. We're all insanely human with foibles galore!

Talk yourself through and out of your anger. Often it's the running dialogue that goes on in our head that fuels the frustration and anger we feel. But you can put the kibosh on this by speaking truth and reminding yourself out loud of things such as this: "My children really aren't out to ruin my life." (Hey! I guarantee you'll need to repeat this little ditty more than once.) State the facts of how you're feeling. "I'm having a miserable day but getting hacked off with my children isn't going to make things better."

Go slow and soft. Okay, this is probably the best and most important bit of advice in the entire book. Seriously. It took my losing my voice completely with laryngitis one Labor Day weekend to realize this wondrous fact. I was homeschooling at the time, teaching two of my children and trying to corral their two-year-old brother. Unable to speak with anything more than the barest whisper, I instructed my children what to do ... and they did it. I corrected them ... and they stopped their obnoxious behavior. A miracle I tell you, a miracle!

Just remember this, it's quite difficult to explode or chew out a child (or an adult for that matter) when speaking in soft, restrained tones.

Lighten up and laugh ... but hold off on the sarcasm. Sometimes moms would rather roll over and die than allow humor to dispel an otherwise stressful situation. Come on, girls, it's time to lighten up and let our children see our laugh lines and hear their mother guffaw and even snort with glee. In fact, pick up one of the accompanying books in this series: *Every Mother Deserves a Good Laugh*, and discover laughter for yourself!

Think ahead about potentially angst-ridden, anger-producing situations. Prepare yourself mentally for circumstances that tend to push your buttons—and plan some type of workable strategy for defusing the situation.

Take the holidays for instance. Some of you reading these pages all but have your head explode when dealing with multiple family visits, meals, and the accompanying packing, loading, and unloading of baby/toddler-related paraphernalia. If this describes you, then consider staying home with your family (husband and kids) and plan your arrival and departure according to what's best for the temperaments and needs of those you love. I know this is quite subversive and I realize grandmothers across the globe may picket in protest at their local bookstore. However, it is what it is, and only you can decide what is best.

Don't overlook the possible need for help with your anger. A counselor with expertise in anger management can help. So can enrolling in a seminar or workshop on assertiveness training. (As crazy as it sounds, a lack of effective assertiveness may be your problem when expressing your emotions.)

Establish and teach your child clear guidelines for expressing anger in a healthy manner. One day I found myself yelling the following at one of my angry children: "Don't look at me that way! Don't you dare stomp up those stairs! Don't speak to me in that tone of voice! Don't you roll your eyes at me!"

At one point the child just stopped and looked at me as if to say, "Good grief, Mom, how am I supposed to show you I'm feeling angry?"

Good point. Here's what I've learned over the years. Instead of cutting off every single expression of irritation and such, establish boundaries in which your children may express their anger (and it's often justified) toward you, their siblings, or life in general.

Encourage them to express their frustration without using the word *you*. "Stop bugging me!" rather than "You bug me." Or "Leave me alone; that makes me angry," rather than "You always make me mad!"

Teach them to talk themselves through times of anger. "I can control my anger," is something every young child can begin repeating when angry. And never forget they will do exactly as you do, so practice what you teach.

Give yourself a time-out. Go to a movie. Buy a new book and curl up and read it cover to cover. Get a pedicure/manicure. Do some gardening. Play the piano. Swing in a hammock. Bake homemade cinnamon rolls. Call your husband and meet him for a "nooner." Exercise (I've been told this is quite enjoyable too). Take another mom out for lunch and do not talk about your kids, your weight, or your husband (or lack thereof). Write a letter to a friend. Catch up on emails to people you really like. Do nothing—absolutely nothing.

Never forget the good days. Today may have been crazy, and your nerves may be frayed. But remember, it's not always like this. There are also those still moments when your little one settles in for the night. Remember tender hugs and kisses that come at the most unexpected moments. Don't forget the soft whispers of affection just before your child drifts off to sleep. Hard as it is to believe in the crisis moments of any given day, that quiet calm will come again.

My day winds to a gentle repose.

*An oft-handled blanket and the soothing power of warm
milk caress my fourteen-month-old with familiarity.*

*Whispered refrains of "Hushabye, don't you cry," bring his
valiant yet futile attempts of wakefulness to quiet defeat. The
weight of his body—amazingly molded against my breast—
is now eased to his bed. Awaiting his presence are stuffed
bunnies and a quilt once possessed by a missed grandmother.*

*I stand—bending and straining, waiting
for the sound all mothers anticipate.*

*Slowly he releases a deep sigh, followed
by the steady and comforting breath of life.*

A prayer is given, thanksgiving for this one, safe and loved.

*Floorboards of creaking pine trumpet my arrival into yet
another realm of motherhood. Sheets are strewn from bedpost
to bedpost—clamped within the power of a closed chest of
drawers. All giving testimony to a day filled
with giggles and childish delight.*

*"We're hiding, Mommy," they scream, followed
by the hearty laughter of brother and sister.*

*I find myself besieged. Ferociously wrestled to the carpet and
pinned, to the cheer of all. Truly a day well spent!*

*Evening rituals begin. Water drains hesitantly from our
ancient tub and plumbing. Kristen and Ricky Neal leave
a trail of dampened footprints as they hurriedly dress and
plunge beneath the pleasantness of freshly laundered sheets.
They find themselves gently encumbered by the weight of
down comforters and hand-sewn quilts.*

*As they snuggle in deep, the tops of their eyelids
barely visible, I pray.*

*I praise the Father of all creation for these three children—
bone of my bone, flesh of my flesh.*

*Mandatory hugs and fishy kisses are doled out; then I retreat,
slowly, creaking floors declaring my exit.*

I turn and hear a soft whisper: "Love you, Mommy."

Perhaps the cover of this book caught your eye on a Store-Mart shelf, grocery store kiosk, or library display. Maybe a mothers' group or book club you participate in chose it as their monthly pick, or you found it lying beneath a pile of stacked reference materials in your physician's waiting room. Perhaps someone purchased it *for* you and/or recommended it *to* you and, given the title, you're just not quite sure what to think. Or perhaps you simply picked it up because it aptly describes where you have been or the place in which you currently find yourself as a mom.

No matter the path that brought you, I'm so glad you came.

I tried my best to create a quick-to-read layout, easy to digest and easy to go to as a reference point in time(s) of need. I included all sorts of quotable quotes that you can tuck away in your memory and use as encouragement for yourself and others, as well as truth found in the Bible.

You see, this one thing I know to be true: change—true and lasting change for our weaknesses, failings, weariness, and worries—can and will ultimately come as the result of truth penetrating our heart.

I know from raw personal experience that it is impossible to change oneself by self-will alone—at least any lasting change. Oh, we can vow to "do better" and all that jazz but eventually, well, eventually we find ourselves back to square one because we're altogether human and finite and limited.

But the truth of Scripture penetrating our heart brings about an entirely different result. When we hear and accept the truth of God's Word, it changes our heart—the core of who we are, how we feel, how we act, and what we believe—and when our heart changes, our thoughts change. And when our thoughts change, our actions change. And when our thoughts and our actions change, our words and feelings change.

And it is then, my sweet friend, that you see lasting change in yourself and in your family.

So if you rushed through or ignored those important words that I quoted from other people or from the Bible, I want to encourage you to go back and reread their wisdom. You may even want to grab a few of those infamous Post-its and mark two or three of your favorites.

Read through them and ask God to show you a particular verse by which you may find comfort, grace, teaching, and change. Copy it and post it near the places you frequent: kitchen, bathroom, baby's changing station, and minivan. Post it, read it aloud, believe it, and live for yourself the truth it contains.

I hope my own confessions of shared struggles and countless discoveries of hope and change along the way helped you feel less alone. I am more convinced each year I live, write, and speak with women that hearing and reading the unvarnished truth of someone else's story is paramount to our believing we are not the only ones battling and struggling.

And last but not least, I hope the personalized prayers touched your mothering heart and spirit. I get to do a lot of amazing things and have traveled across the world—literally—but time and time again this consistency remains: I find praying for individuals, one-on-one, undoubtedly to be my favorite thing to do. As you pray, I'd like you to imagine me standing with you—in front of you with my left hand placed on your right shoulder and my right gently pressed against the back of your neck. Our heads bowed—foreheads leaning toward one another—as we simply talk real with God about our needs and His ability to meet them.

That's all.

No fill-in-the-blanks.

No tests or teaching points to ponder.

It's just you and me touching base in the most meaningful and relaxed manner I know. So enjoy, my friend, and know I'm cheering for you from across the miles—cheering and praying peace, joy, contentment, and confidence in your life as a woman and mom. I'll look forward to hearing from you personally as a result of our time together.

Until then!

Julie

Julie Barnhill
julie@juliebarnhill.com
onetoughmothertalk.blogspot.com

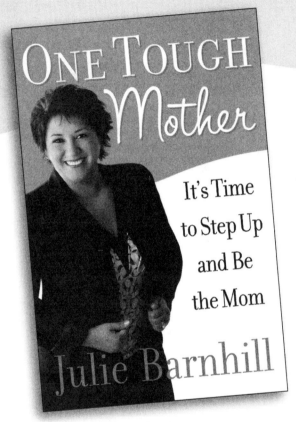

from Author
Julie Barnhill

EVERY
MOTHER
CAN
Beat the Blues

Julie Barnhill
AUTHOR OF ONE TOUGH MOTHER

EVERY
MOTHER
DESERVES
a Good Laugh

Julie Barnhill
AUTHOR OF ONE TOUGH MOTHER

EVERY
MOTHER
CAN
Let Go of Stress

Julie Barnhill
AUTHOR OF ONE TOUGH MOTHER

EVERY
MOTHER
CAN
Keep Her Cool

Julie Barnhill
AUTHOR OF ONE TOUGH MOTHER

MOPS
Mothers of Preschoolers

Better together...

MOPS is here to come alongside you
during this season of early mothering to
give you the support and resources you
need to be a great mom.

Get connected today!